Praying with Power
A Prayer Journal

Jill C.Power

Teresa ~
May God bless the
work of your hands, and
may He guide your
every step.
♡ Jill

DEDICATION

For my husband, John.
Thank you for supporting my God-sized dreams.

ACKNOWLEDGMENTS

God has placed some amazing people in my life, people who love me and encourage me. People who wouldn't let me stop even when I felt overwhelmed and unsure. Foremost, my husband, John. Thank you for supporting me in every situation. Thank you for believing in me when I didn't believe in myself. Thank you for reminding me about the importance of being obedient.

To our children, Aaron, Adam, and Avery—your love and support melts my heart. You will never know how much it means to me to hear you say, "Mom, we are proud of you." I hope I taught you to listen for His voice, and to follow His lead.

To my family: Mamaw, Papaw, James, Joni, Butch, Nan, Tyler, Jake, Jayden, and Taylor W. Thank you for supporting me, being my first blog followers, and for praying for me always.

To all my friends who supported and encouraged me: I love you!

Special thanks to my editor, Lori. Thank you for believing in my writing and the message I wanted to share. Thanks to Bernadette, Diamond, Tammy, Deborah, Melinda, and Stacey for being an extra set of eyes. Thank you, Mandy, for the beautiful cover photo and setting. Thank you, Misti, for saving my sanity with 300 dpi!

A special shout out to all of the pastors of Stonewater Church. Thank you for teaching me that a relationship with Jesus is more important than following rules. Thank you for showing me how to listen for God's voice, and how to obey His words.

I want to thank my Community Group Members: Jeff, Celeste, Kelly, Kyle, Phillip, Stacey, April, Randy, Paul, and Mandy. I love doing life with each of you!

Most importantly, thank you Lord for trusting me to share this message. I am constantly humbled by your grace and goodness. We serve an amazing God!

Several years ago, I started a morning routine that has deepened my relationship with God more than anything else I've ever done. I started getting up earlier than my family, and spending quiet time alone with God. We see this modeled by Jesus in Mark. *"And rising very early in the morning, while it was still dark, he (Jesus) departed and went out to a desolate place, and there he prayed. And Simon and those who were with him searched for him, and they found him and said, 'Everyone is looking for you.'"* (Mark 1:35-37) If Jesus needs time alone to speak to the Father, then surely we do too!

In the beginning, I would go into this time with a list of things to talk about, and my own personal agenda. I mean, I am a teacher/mom/wife—my life revolves around lists! However, after a few weeks, I changed my approach to quiet time.

I started my quiet time with a prayer where I would ask God to show me what He has planned for me that day. After all, this time together should be more about Him leading me. I still pray this exact prayer, "Lord, what would you like me to do in this time we have together?"

I must admit that in those first few weeks, I felt very inadequate when it came to praying. I know that prayer is one of the most valuable things we can do in our walk with God, but it's also very intimidating. I've listened to others pray with such eloquence, and I've wondered what God thought of my meager little attempts to communicate with Him. Does God want me to speak to Him in a certain way? Is there a right way to pray? What if I don't know what to say?

Again, the Bible answers all the questions!

Where should we pray?

We can pray anywhere, and at any time! God is always listening. In Matthew, Jesus teaches his disciples (us) that prayer is something sacred between us and God. *"But when you pray, go into your room, close the door and pray to your Father, who is unseen. Then your Father, who sees what is done in secret will reward you. And when you pray, do not keep babbling like pagans, for they think they will be heard because of their many words. Do not be like them, for your Father knows what you need before you ask Him."* (Matthew 6: 6-7)

Here is my interpretation of the above scripture:
- Find a quiet place to pray. This is one reason I get up earlier in the mornings than my family. It's hard for me to concentrate and give focus to God with distractions. I also don't say my in-depth prayers in bed at night. It's hard to admit, but if it's too quiet, and I'm too still, I will fall asleep while talking to God.
- In biblical times, people believed the bigger the words, and the longer the prayer, the more likely God would listen. Actually, God wants the exact opposite. God already knows our heart, so He wants honesty and sincerity. There is no pressure to use the "right" words—we just need to speak what we really feel.

How should we pray?

Jesus provides us with a model for prayer. It is an example of what our prayers should contain. Does that mean that every prayer should follow this pattern? Absolutely not! Remember, prayer is a conversation with God. A quick prayer during the middle of the day probably won't follow this model, nor will a prayer full of thanksgiving. There are times when my prayers are only cries to God in desperation, and there are other times when I just sit and listen for God's voice in my heart. Generally, however, I pray following these guidelines in Matthew 6: 9-13 KJV. (Bold letters are the verses, while italics are my interpretation).

"This then is how you should pray; 'Our Father which art in heaven, hallowed be thy name, *(Address God with the reverence and honor He deserves.)* **Thy kingdom come, Thy will be done in earth as it is in heaven.** *(Pray that God's will be done. Not MY will, but HIS.)* **Give us this day our daily bread.** *(Ask God for what I need.)* **And forgive us our debts, as we forgive our debtors.** *(Forgive me of my sins, just as I must forgive others.)* **And lead us not into temptation, but deliver us from the evil one.** *(Please help me avoid sin, and keep me safe from attacks from the devil.)* **For thine is the kingdom, and the power, and the glory forever.** *(All glory be to God for His love and strength. You are my King!)* **Amen.**

Why should we pray?

The Bible is full of verses pointing to the importance and need of prayer, but here are two of my favorites.

- *"Is anyone among you in trouble? Let them pray. Is anyone happy? Let them sing songs of praise. Is anyone among you sick? Let them call the elders of the church to pray over them and anoint them with oil in the name of the Lord."* (James 5:13-14)
- *"Therefore confess your sins to each other and pray for each other so that you may be healed. The prayer of a righteous person is powerful and effective."* (James 5:16)

It's also important to remember, prayer is not just you talking to God, but also waiting on an answer. *"Let all that I am wait quietly before God, for my hope is in Him. He alone is my rock and my salvation, my fortress where I will not be shaken."* (Psalm 62: 5-6)

What if I just don't know what to say to God?

I have those moments too! In those times when we absolutely don't know what to say, the Bible tells us in Romans 8:26, *"In the same way the Spirit helps us in our weakness. We don't know what we ought to pray for, but the Spirit himself intercedes for us through wordless groans."* Ask the Holy Spirit to guide you in your prayers!

I remember when I started getting serious about my prayer life, my prayers were simple, to the point, and did not contain much depth. As I have spent more time with God in prayer, and in His word, my prayers have matured. My relationship with God has deepened, and so have our conversations!

I've found it very helpful to write down my prayers. Writing helps me to stay focused, to make sure I haven't forgotten something, and to hold myself accountable for spending time with God in prayer. I created this prayer journal as a way to deepen my relationship with Jesus. Hopefully, it will deepen yours too. I always love looking back over my written prayers to see how God has answered them—even if the answer looks different than what I expected!

Here are some ideas and suggestions for developing and maintaining your own personal time with God:

- Make your quiet time a priority. Schedule it on your daily calendar, or make it the first thing you do every day.
- Create a space in your home for it. It could be your closet, an empty bedroom, your office, or the kitchen table. Have your journal, something to write with, and your Bible with you.

- Make time to listen. Don't just talk to God—some days you also need to sit still and listen to His voice. I've found that His voice starts in my heart and then moves into my head.
- Find a friend to walk alongside of you. You can share what you are learning in your quiet time, and you can be a source of encouragement to one another.

How do you use the journal?

Each week of this journal starts with a focus verse. These 52 verses are some of my favorites! After the verse, you will find one or two guiding questions about the verse. There is space after the verse where I encourage you to use these questions to think more deeply about what that particular scripture means to you.

After that, you will see six areas of prayer focus for the week: faith, family, friends, feelings, finances, and other. You can complete one focus area per day, or pray about several of them in one day. Want to start your week on a Wednesday? Great! The journal is designed to be adaptable to your needs, so do whatever works best for you!

Along with the focus areas, I've included a place for asking forgiveness, offering thanksgiving, and an additional blank area where you can continue writing about things that God is placing on your heart.

Just a quick additional note: Your prayers do not have to relate to the focus verse. The focus verse is there to help you interact with the scriptures.

I am so glad that you are joining me on this journey to deepen our walk with God. I will be using this same journal too! Start by committing ten minutes a day to talking with God, and then be open to where God leads you. I'm praying for you, and I hope that you will pray for me too!

Unless noted, all verses are the New International Version (NIV) of the Bible.

Prayer Categories
Use this page if you need help with your prayers each week.

Faith: *Anything that goes with your faith: church, general prayers, things hoped for, things testing your faith, salvation*

Family: *Family members: health, salvation, guidance, protection, unity, jobs, travel. Name your family members and their specific need.*

Friends: *Anything that goes with your friends: pursuing Godly friends, individual needs of your friends, protection, unity, jobs. Name your friend with their specific need.*

Feelings: *Pray that your feelings would be based on scripture, protecting your heart, personal issues, fears/insecurities. Are you hurting or happy?*

Finances: *How is God working in your finances? Are you honoring Him through your finances? Has God given you extra blessings that are meant to be shared? Do you need His help in your finances?*

Other: *Are there any other concerns you would like to bring before God this week? Prayers for: country, leaders, morality. What can you do to please and honor God?*

What are your goals for using this prayer journal?
Write them down, and refer back to them throughout the year.

Be still and know that I am God.
Psalm 46:10

- What does it mean to "be still and know?"
- Why is it so hard to be still?

Week of: _____

Response:

Faith:

Family:

Friends:

Feelings:

Finances:

Other:

Thank you, Lord…

Forgive me, Lord…

.

Many are the plans in a person's heart, but it is the Lord's purpose that prevails.
Proverbs 19:21

- Have there been times when you didn't like the Lord's plan?
- Why is it better for His plan to prevail?

Week of: _____

Response:

Faith:

Family:

Friends:

Feelings:

Finances:

Other:

Thank you, Lord...

Forgive me, Lord...

Come to me all who are weary and heavy-laden, and I will give you rest.
Matthew 11:28

- What heavy burdens are you carrying around?
- Picture giving all these burdens to Jesus, and then falling into His arms! How would that feel?

Week of: _____

Response:

Faith:

Family:

Friends:

Feelings:

Finances:

Other:

Thank you, Lord...

Forgive me, Lord...
.

So whether you eat or drink or whatever you do, do all to the glory of God.
1 Corinthians 10:31

- How can food and drink bring glory to God?
- How can you use this verse to bring glory to God this week?

Week of: _____

Response:

Faith:

Family:

Friends:

Feelings:

Finances:

Other:

Thank you, Lord...

Forgive me, Lord...

For wherever your treasure is, there your heart will be also.
Luke 12:34

- On what do you spend the most money?
- Does how you spend your money glorify the Lord?

Week of: _____

Response:

Faith:

Family:

Friends:

Feelings:

Finances:

Other:

Thank you, Lord…

Forgive me, Lord…

.

And now these three remain: faith, hope, and love. But the greatest of these is love.
1 Corinthians 13:13

- Why is love the greatest of these?
- How do you show love to others?

Week of: _____

Response:

Faith:

Family:

Friends:

Feelings:

Finances:

Other:

Thank you, Lord…

Forgive me, Lord…

.

Be kind and compassionate to one another, forgiving each other, just as God in Christ forgave you.
Ephesians 4:32

- Is there someone you need to forgive, or someone from whom you need to seek forgiveness?
- Pray and ask God to help you!

Week of: _____

Response:

Faith:

Family:

Friends:

Feelings:

Finances:

Other:

Thank you, Lord…

Forgive me, Lord…

.

And whatever you do, whether in word or deed, do it all in the name of the Lord Jesus, giving thanks to God the Father through him.
Colossians 3:17

- What is an area in your life in which you need to give God thanks?
- Are there areas of your life that might improve if you thought about doing it all in the name of Jesus?

Week of: _____

Response:

Faith:

Family:

Friends:

Feelings:

Finances:

Other:

Thank you, Lord…

Forgive me, Lord…
.

Be strong and courageous. Do not be afraid or discouraged. For the
Lord your God is with you wherever you go.
Joshua 1:9

- What scares you?
- How might your life be different if you asked God to be
  with you in each of these areas?

Week of: _____

Response:

Faith:

Family:

Friends:

Feelings:

Finances:

Other:

Thank you, Lord…

Forgive me, Lord…

And the Lord came and called as before "Samuel, Samuel." And Samuel replied, "Speak, your servant is listening."
1 Samuel 3:10

- In what ways can God speak to you?
- How do you know when God is speaking to you?

Week of: _____

Response:

Faith:

Family:

Friends:

Feelings:

Finances:

Other:

Thank you, Lord…

Forgive me, Lord…
.

But God demonstrated his own love for us in this: While we were still sinners, Christ died for us.
Romans 5:8

- Does Jesus expect us to be perfect in order to be saved?
- How does it feel to know that Jesus died for you?

Week of: _____

Response:

Faith:

Family:

Friends:

Feelings:

Finances:

Other:

Thank you, Lord…

Forgive me, Lord…

.

Trust in the Lord with all your heart and lean not on your own understanding; in all your ways submit to him, and he will make your path straight.
Proverbs 3:5

- Why do we need to trust the Lord and submit to Him?
- In what areas of your life are you most tempted to lean on your own understanding instead of trusting God?

Week of: _____

Response:

Faith:

Family:

Friends:

Feelings:

Finances:

Other:

Thank you, Lord...

Forgive me, Lord...
·

"For I know the plans I have for you," declares the Lord, "plans to prosper you and not to harm you, plans to give you hope and a future."
Jeremiah 29:11

- Do you believe God plans a hope and future for you?
- Ask God to guide you to follow His plan.

Week of: _____

Response:

Faith:

Family:

Friends:

Feelings:

Finances:

Other:

Thank you, Lord…

Forgive me, Lord…
.

And we know that in all things God works for the good of those who love him, who have been called according to his purpose.
Romans 8:28

- Have you thought about what it really means to love the Lord?
- Have you allowed yourself to be called to His purpose?

Week of: _____

Response:

Faith:

Family:

Friends:

Feelings:

Finances:

Other:

Thank you, Lord…

Forgive me, Lord…

.

And my God will meet all your needs according to the riches of his glory in Christ Jesus.
Philippians 4:19

- What does the "riches of his glory" mean, and how can they meet your needs?
- How does God want to meet your needs?

Week of: _____

Response:

Faith:

Family:

Friends:

Feelings:

Finances:

Other:

Thank you, Lord…

Forgive me, Lord…

.

Greater love has no one than this: to lay down one's life for one's friends.
John 15:13

- In what ways would you be willing to sacrifice for a friend?
- How about an enemy?

Week of: _____

Response:

Faith:

Family:

Friends:

Feelings:

Finances:

Other:

Thank you, Lord...

Forgive me, Lord...
.

Commit to the Lord whatever you do, and he will establish your plans.
Proverbs 16:3

- • What does it look like to commit your plans to the Lord?
- • What plans do you have that you haven't yet prayed for?

Week of: _____

Response:

Faith:

Family:

Friends:

Feelings:

Finances:

Other:

Thank you, Lord…

Forgive me, Lord…

.

Do everything in love.
1 Corinthians 16:14

- What is one way you can show God's love this week?
- What is something you find difficult to do in love?

Week of: _____

Response:

Faith:

Family:

Friends:

Feelings:

Finances:

Other:

Thank you, Lord...

Forgive me, Lord...

·

I will extol the Lord at all times; his praise will always be on my lips.
Psalm 34:1

- What are you praising the Lord for this week?
- Can you also praise Him during adversity?

Week of: _____

Response:

Faith:

Family:

Friends:

Feelings:

Finances:

Other:

Thank you, Lord...

Forgive me, Lord...

.

Charm is deceitful and beauty is fleeting; but a woman who fears the Lord is to be praised.
Proverbs 31:30

- Are you more concerned with your outward or your inward beauty?
- What does it mean to have true reverence for the Lord?

Week of: _____

Response:

Faith:

Family:

Friends:

Feelings:

Finances:

Other:

Thank you, Lord…

Forgive me, Lord…

In the same way, let your light shine before others, that they may see your good deeds and glorify your Father in heaven.
Matthew 5:16

- Do you believe that your actions can bring glory to God?
- Are you handling situations in a way that allows others to see God in you?

Week of: _____

Response:

Faith:

Family:

Friends:

Feelings:

Finances:

Other:

Thank you, Lord…

Forgive me, Lord…

.

Jesus looked at them and said, "With man this is impossible, but not with God; all things are possible with God."
Mark 10:27

- What has God done for you that man could not?
- Praise God for all that He has done!

Week of: _____

Response:

Faith:

Family:

Friends:

Feelings:

Finances:

Other:

Thank you, Lord…

Forgive me, Lord…

For God did not send his Son into the world to condemn the world, but to save the world through him.
John 3:17

- This verse follows the famous John 3:16.
- What does this mean to how you live your daily life?

Week of: _____

Response:

Faith:

Family:

Friends:

Feelings:

Finances:

Other:

Thank you, Lord…

Forgive me, Lord…
.

He must become greater; I must become less.
John 3:30

- How can you make Jesus "greater" in your life?
- What areas of your life do you struggle to control, and how successful do you think you are?

Week of: _____

Response:

Faith:

Family:

Friends:

Feelings:

Finances:

Other:

Thank you, Lord…

Forgive me, Lord…

.

Offer hospitality to one another without grumbling.
1 Peter 4:9

- • What is one way you can show hospitality this week?
- • Why is it sometimes hard to help without complaint?

Week of: _____

Response:

Faith:

Family:

Friends:

Feelings:

Finances:

Other:

Thank you, Lord…

Forgive me, Lord…

Therefore encourage one another and build each other up, just as in fact you are doing.
1 Thessalonians 5:11

- What does it mean to encourage and build each other up?
- Who needs encouragement from you?

Week of: _____

Response:

Faith:

Family:

Friends:

Feelings:

Finances:

Other:

Thank you, Lord…

Forgive me, Lord…

Whatever you do, work at it with all your heart, as working for the Lord, not for human masters...
Colossians 3:23

- How would it be different if you worked each day as though you were working for the Lord?
- What is one thing you can do differently this week?

Week of: _____

Response:

Faith:

Family:

Friends:

Feelings:

Finances:

Other:

Thank you, Lord…

Forgive me, Lord…

.

Do not be anxious about anything, but in every situation, by prayer and petitions, with thanksgiving, present your requests to God.
Philippians 4:6

- What worries keep you up at night?
- Thank God for all He has done in the past, and then turn your requests over to Him.

Week of: _____

Response:

Faith:

Family:

Friends:

Feelings:

Finances:

Other:

Thank you, Lord…

Forgive me, Lord…

Each of you should use whatever gifts you have received to serve others as faithful stewards of God's grace.
1 Peter 4:10

- What kind of gift do you think God has given you?
- How can you use it to serve others?

Week of: _____

Response:

Faith:

Family:

Friends:

Feelings:

Finances:

Other:

Thank you, Lord…

Forgive me, Lord…

.

How great you are Sovereign Lord! There is no one like you, and there is no God but you, as we have heard with our own ears.
2 Samuel 7:22

- What makes the Lord so great?
- Ask God to remind you of all the ways He has revealed His greatness to you, and then sing His praises!

Week of: _____

Response:

Faith:

Family:

Friends:

Feelings:

Finances:

Other:

Thank you, Lord…

Forgive me, Lord…

·

For you created my inmost being; you knit me together in my mother's womb.
Psalm 139:13

- God created you from the very beginning. If there are things about yourself that you struggle to appreciate, ask God to help you see yourself as He sees you.

Week of: _____

Response:

Faith:

Family:

Friends:

Feelings:

Finances:

Other:

Thank you, Lord…

Forgive me, Lord…
.

No one can serve two masters. Either you will hate the one and love the other, or you will be devoted to one and despise the other. You cannot serve both God and money.
Matthew 6:24

- What does it mean to serve money?
- Why can you not be devoted to both God and money?

Week of: _____

Response:

Faith:

Family:

Friends:

Feelings:

Finances:

Other:

Thank you, Lord…

Forgive me, Lord…

Each of you should give what you have decided in your heart to give, not reluctantly under compulsion, for God loves a cheerful giver.
2 Corinthians 9:7

- Have you ever given and then complained about it?
- Why does God want us to give with a cheerful heart?

Week of: _____

Response:

Faith:

Family:

Friends:

Feelings:

Finances:

Other:

Thank you, Lord...

Forgive me, Lord...

.

All scripture is God-breathed and is useful for teaching, rebuking, correcting, and training in righteousness, so that the servant of God may be thoroughly equipped for every good work.
2 Timothy 3:16-17

- How can scripture help you be equipped for every good work?

Week of: _____

Response:

Faith:

Family:

Friends:

Feelings:

Finances:

Other:

Thank you, Lord...

Forgive me, Lord...

.

God is not unjust; he will not forget your work and the love you have shown him as you have helped his people and continue to help them.
Hebrew 6:10

- Why is it so important to God that we help others?
- During prayer, ask God to show you who needs your help.

Week of: _____

Response:

Faith:

Family:

Friends:

Feelings:

Finances:

Other:

Thank you, Lord…

Forgive me, Lord…
.

The Lord is not slow in keeping his promise, as some understand slowness. Instead he is patient with you, not wanting anyone to perish, but everyone to come to repentance.
2 Peter 3:9

- Do you know someone who has not accepted Jesus as their personal savior?
- Pray every day this week for God to present an opportunity for you to reach out to this person.

Week of: _____

Response:

Faith:

Family:

Friends:

Feelings:

Finances:

Other:

Thank you, Lord…

Forgive me, Lord…

.

Dear children, let us not love with words and speech but in actions and truth.
1 John 3:18

- Why are our actions more important to God than our words?
- Where can you show God's love this week?

Week of: _____

Response:

Faith:

Family:

Friends:

Feelings:

Finances:

Other:

Thank you, Lord…

Forgive me, Lord…

.

If any of you lacks wisdom, you should ask God, who gives generously to all without finding fault, and it will be given to you.
James 1:5

- In what area of your life do you need God's wisdom?
- Be faithful in bringing that request to Him!

Week of: _____

Response:

Faith:

Family:

Friends:

Feelings:

Finances:

Other:

Thank you, Lord…

Forgive me, Lord…

Am I now trying to win the approval of human beings, or of God? Or am I trying to please people? If I were still trying to please people, I would not be a servant of God.
Galatians 1:10

- Why is it more important to please God?
- Are there areas of your life where you struggle to please people?

Week of: _____

Response:

Faith:

Family:

Friends:

Feelings:

Finances:

Other:

Thank you, Lord…

Forgive me, Lord…

The heart is deceitful above all things and beyond cure. Who can understand it?
Jeremiah 17:9

- We tend to say things like "Follow your heart." Why does God warn against that?
- What can you rely on for direction instead of your heart?

Week of: _____

Response:

Faith:

Family:

Friends:

Feelings:

Finances:

Other:

Thank you, Lord…

Forgive me, Lord…

My dear brothers and sisters, take note of this: Everyone should be quick to listen, slow to speak, and slow to become angry.
James 1:19

- Which of the above do you battle most, and how can God help you?
- Write a quick prayer you can call upon in these situations.

Week of: _____

Response:

Faith:

Family:

Friends:

Feelings:

Finances:

Other:

Thank you, Lord…

Forgive me, Lord…

.

*Be alert and of sober mind. Your enemy the devil prowls around like a
roaring lion looking for someone to devour.*
1 Peter 5:8

- Why does the Devil want to destroy you?
- In what areas of your life do you feel vulnerable to his attacks?

Week of: _____

Response:

Faith:

Family:

Friends:

Feelings:

Finances:

Other:

Thank you, Lord...

Forgive me, Lord...

.

Love the Lord your God with all your heart and with all your soul and with all your strength.
Deuteronomy 6:5

- We tend to use the word "love" freely: you love your car, coffee, or your new shoes. What does it really look like to love the Lord in the way described?
- How would things be different if you loved God in this way?

Week of: _____

Response:

Faith:

Family:

Friends:

Feelings:

Finances:

Other:

Thank you, Lord…

Forgive me, Lord…
·

I have hidden your word in my heart that I might not sin against you.
Psalm 119:11

- What are some of your favorite Bible verses?
- What are some Bible verses that can help you in areas where you are tempted to sin? Ask God to show you!

Week of: _____

Response:

Faith:

Family:

Friends:

Feelings:

Finances:

Other:

Thank you, Lord…

Forgive me, Lord…

Then you will call on me and come and pray to me, and I will listen to you. You will seek me and find me when you seek me with all your heart.
Jeremiah 29:12-13

- What does it look like to give your whole heart to God?
- What is keeping you from it?

Week of: _____

Response:

Faith:

Family:

Friends:

Feelings:

Finances:

Other:

Thank you, Lord…

Forgive me, Lord…

.

"Ask and it will be given to you; seek and you will find; knock and the door will be opened to you."
Matthew 7:7

- God tells us again and again to bring our requests to Him. What is deep in your heart that you want to ask of Him?

Week of: _____

Response:

Faith:

Family:

Friends:

Feelings:

Finances:

Other:

Thank you, Lord…

Forgive me, Lord…

.

On hearing this, Jesus said to them, "It is not the healthy who need a doctor, but the sick. I have not come to call the righteous, but sinners."
Mark 2:17

- Do you have an area of sin that keeps plaguing you?
- I challenge you to ask Jesus for help in this area!

Week of: _____

Response:

Faith:

Family:

Friends:

Feelings:

Finances:

Other:

Thank you, Lord…

Forgive me, Lord…

.

But the fruit of the Spirit is love, joy, peace, forbearance, kindness, goodness, faithfulness, gentleness, and self-control. Against such things there is no law.
Galatians 5:22-23

- Where do these "fruits" come from?
- Have you seen any of these increase as a result of prayer time?

Week of: _____

Response:

Faith:

Family:

Friends:

Feelings:

Finances:

Other:

Thank you, Lord...

Forgive me, Lord...

No temptation has overtaken you except what is common to mankind. And God is faithful; he will not let you be tempted beyond what you can bear.
1 Corinthians 10:13

- When you are tempted, have you asked God to provide a way out?
- What tempts you most?

Week of: _____

Response:

Faith:

Family:

Friends:

Feelings:

Finances:

Other:

Thank you, Lord…

Forgive me, Lord…

.

And if we know that he hears us—whatever we ask—we know that we have what we asked of him.
1 John 5:15

- What is a prayer that God granted you?
- Has there been a prayer that was answered differently than what you expected?

Week of: _____

Response:

Faith:

Family:

Friends:

Feelings:

Finances:

Other:

Thank you, Lord...

Forgive me, Lord...

Jesus Christ is the same yesterday and today and forever.
Hebrews 13:8

- How is Christ the same today, over 2,000 years after His birth?
- What have you learned about Jesus during this time?

Week of: _____

Response:

Faith:

Family:

Friends:

Feelings:

Finances:

Other:

Thank you, Lord…

Forgive me, Lord…
.

What next?

It is my sincere hope that your relationship with Jesus has deepened significantly over the course of using this journal. I encourage you to:

- Look back over the journal. Note places where God answered prayers. (Even if the answer looks differently than you expected!)
- Circle some of the verses you would like to commit to memory.
- Are there areas where you would like to continue praying?

Having an authentic relationship with God doesn't require you to be perfect, or to follow a specific set of rules. In my life, there have been three main things that have helped me continue to grow as a Christian.

Love.

"He (Jesus) answered, 'Love the Lord your God with all your heart and with all your soul and with all your strength and with all your mind; and 'Love your neighbor as yourself.'" (Luke 10:27)

"Above all, love each other deeply, because love covers a multitude of sins." (1 Peter 4:8)

It is important that you love God more than anything else. That means even more than your spouse, more than your kids, and more than your friends. Just like any relationship in your life, our relationship with God flourishes the more time we spend with Him. In my experience, the more time I spend with God through prayer and reading my Bible, the more I get to know His heart, and the deeper my love is for Him.

If you are married, or in a committed relationship, think back to the beginning. Did you love that person with the kind of love you do now? Probably not, because real love takes time to develop.

Pray.

As I said in the beginning of the prayer journal, my relationship with God changed dramatically as I took time to go to Him each day in prayer. Along with reading my Bible, prayer allowed me to really get to know God. For the first time in my life, I truly felt that I had a real relationship with our Lord.

Remember that prayer is a conversation. Sometimes you speak, and sometimes you just listen. Don't feel like you have to sit down in a quiet place every time you want to pray. I like to do what I call "text messages to God." Just like I would send a text to my husband or a friend throughout the day, I send quick prayers to God. I try to keep the lines of communication with God open all day long!

You've started a good routine of setting aside time for Him daily. Now I encourage you to keep it up! Make prayer a priority in your life.

If you have finished the prayer journal, and have enjoyed writing down your prayers, find a blank journal or a notebook you would want to use. Writing prayers has always been so much more powerful to me, and I hope you have seen the power in it as well.

Serve.

Loving God and praying are essential pieces to fostering a relationship with God. There are many more spiritual disciplines that can help that relationship mature: fasting, worship, personal reflection, and confession are just a few. For me, the one thing that matured my relationship with God more than any other was service.

"For even the Son of Man did not come to be served, but to serve, and to give his life as a ransom for many." (Mark 10:45) Jesus himself came to earth to serve!

Two of my favorite verses about service are:
- *"Each of you should use whatever gift you have received to serve others, as faithful stewards of God's grace in its various forms."* (1 Peter 4:10)
- *"You, my brothers and sisters, were called to be free. But do not use your freedom to indulge the flesh; rather, serve one another humbly in love."* (Galatians 5:13)

The first place I served at church was in the nursery; after all, I did give birth to three babies at once. Honestly, it was very challenging. It's not easy to know how to calm a crying baby that isn't your own. But, here's the thing, because I was willing to serve in the nursery, it meant a mom and dad were getting to worship in peace. That hour spent in the nursery was HUGE for those parents!

I moved from serving in the nursery to passing out programs as people entered the church service. I love smiling and greeting people, so it was a natural fit. I was able to greet our regular attendees, welcome new people to our church, and hopefully send out the message that each person there was important.

Remember, no act of service is too small or unimportant. The more I served, the more I began loving God's people, and the deeper my relationship with Him grew. For me, it was truly life-changing.

What are your personal strengths or gifts? Use them to serve others, and find a place to serve God. Volunteer in your church. Take your neighbors a meal. Give food to the local food bank. I'm strongly suggesting you get outside of your comfort zone on this one. In the times when you feel inadequate, you will depend more on God's grace and power to help you. Again, Jesus came to serve and so should we.

Accepting Jesus as Your Savior

Some of you reading this prayer journal have not yet accepted Jesus as your personal Savior. Is this something you want to do? Do you feel God reaching out to you to accept Him?

John 3:16 says, *"For God so loved the world that he gave his one and only Son, that whoever believes in him shall not perish but have eternal life."* Do you believe that Jesus came to this earth to die for your sins, and was resurrected back to life after three days? Romans 10:9 says, *"That if you confess with your mouth the Lord Jesus and believe in your heart that God has raised Him from the dead, you will be saved."*

If you would like to be saved by God's grace, write these verses down, or pray them out loud. If you have already professed that Jesus is your Savior, but have not yet been baptized, I encourage you to reach out to a pastor or church member who can help you.

I'm so glad you have joined me on this journey! It is my sincere prayer that each of you have been touched by something you've read, or by something you've experienced with God over the past 52 weeks.

Remember to keep your relationship with God as a priority in your life. May God bless you and keep you.

Love. Pray. Serve.

ABOUT THE AUTHOR

Jill has been married for over twenty years, and is the proud mom to an amazing set of triplets. A teacher by trade, Jill has spent 23 years educating children in public schools. Jill uses her gift of teaching to reach people for Jesus. At her church, she leads pastoral care for women, and she has been authoring a Christian blog for many years. When she is not at church or writing, Jill enjoys traveling with her family, watching football, and pretending like she is a chef at family dinners. She shares her home with her two dogs, Cletus and Bella, and her cat, Pickles.

You can follow Jill at www.jillcpower.com, or
on Facebook at www.facebook.com/reachforjesus.